THE RETURN
OF THE PROPHET

THE RETURN
OF THE PROPHET

HAJJAR GIBRAN

ATRIA BOOKS
New York London Toronto Sydney

BEYOND WORDS
Hillsboro, Oregon

ATRIA BOOKS

A Division of Simon & Schuster, Inc.
1230 Avenue of the Americas
New York, NY 10020

BEYOND WORDS

20827 N.W. Cornell Road, Suite 500
Hillsboro, Oregon 97124-9808
503-531-8700 / 503-531-8773 fax
www.beyondword.com

Managing editor: Lindsay S. Brown
Editor: Julie Steigerwaldt
Copyeditor: Henry Covey
Proofreader: Ali McCart
Illustrations: Alexander Chubotin
Design: Sara E. Blum

First Atria Books/Beyond Words hardcover edition October 2008

ATRIA BOOKS and colophon are trademarks of Simon & Schuster, Inc. Beyond Words Publishing is a division of Simon & Schuster, Inc.

For more information about special discounts for bulk purchases, please contact Simon & Schuster Special Sales at 1-800-456-6798 or business@simonandschuster.com.

Manufactured in the United States of America

10 9 8 7 6 5 4 3 2 1

Library of Congress Cataloging-in-Publication Data:

Gibran, Hajjar.
  The return of the prophet / Hajjar Gibran ; original illustrations by Alexander Chubotin. -- 1st Atria Books/Beyond Words hardcover ed.
    p. cm.
    1. Spiritual life--Poetry. 2. Spiritual life--Meditations. I. Title.
  PS3607.I263R48 2008
  811'.6--dc22

                                                    2008023623

  ISBN-13:   978-1-58270-198-1
  ISBN-10:   1-58270-198-9

The corporate mission of Beyond Words Publishing, Inc.: *Inspire to Integrity*

To my mother,
from whom I inherited the Gibran lineage

And to my family, friends, and teachers,
who guided me through clouds of doubt
so that I may sow these seeds of love

And most dearly to you,
who cherish the spirit of Kahlil's prophet
and keep your heart a home where he may
forever return

CONTENTS

THE PROMISE

Should my voice fade in your ears, and my love vanish in your memory, then I will come again,

And with a richer heart and lips more yielding to the spirit will I speak.

Yea, I shall return with the tide . . .

If aught I have said is truth, that truth shall reveal itself in a clearer voice, and in words more kin to your thoughts . . . .

And if this day is not a fulfillment of your needs and my love, then let it be a promise till another day . . . .

Know, therefore, that from the greater silence I shall return . . . .

A little while, a moment of rest upon the wind, and another woman shall bear me.

—Kahlil Gibran
FROM THE FINAL CHAPTER OF *The Prophet*

INTRODUCTION

When my brother died, my father sobbed; I was silent for several years.

In the aftermath of his death, my mother reached into my sleepless coma and placed a copy of *The Prophet* on my pillow. I opened it and read the first few words. *Almustafa, the chosen and the beloved, who was a dawn unto his own day.* I couldn't even pronounce *Almustafa* let alone understand the string of words that followed.

I threw the book aside and forgot about it.

But let me start at the beginning.

My brother, Gary, was my hero. One year younger, I always stayed one step close behind him. Together we would scamper hand in hand over wooden planks through the vegetable garden that separated our yard from our grandparents'. Our short street ended in an enchanted forest alive with birds and squirrels. Gary and I built stick forts and raced caterpillars in the thick underbrush. Like the strings of two kites soaring in a summer breeze, our lifelines were a tangled unity.

He was also my obliging rival. We wrestled often, and although Gary was much stronger, he never hurt me. He always gave enough slack to fight. I would throw myself at him with all the muscle I could muster, and with enduring patience, he allowed me to exhaust my limits. I felt so safe in his gentle strength.

As we entered adolescence in a shared quest for manhood, we were inseparable.

I was envious when Dad taught Gary how to shoot his rifle. I didn't know then that it was to be our undoing.

Out rabbit hunting with a friend, Gary slipped on a patch of ice and dropped his rifle; on impact it fired a bullet through his heart.

In that unthinkable flash, his life was snuffed out.

Without him everything seemed meaningless.

Our family was in shock, but I hardly noticed; the anguish was too much for me to feel. I was numb, unable to speak or cry. At home, I preferred to be alone in the room we had shared, even though it felt like a graveyard of living memories. I used to lie under his upper bunk and bounce him up with my legs. If I pushed him too far he'd jump out of bed with a huge smile, wrestle me to the floor, and torture me with tickles. Now I lay staring at the upper bunk with only the weight of Gary's absence sinking in.

I didn't look anyone in the eyes for shame they would see my desperation. And though I rarely spoke, I kept busy to avoid the pain. I dreamt about girls and fast cars, and both seemed to constantly get me in trouble. I fell in with the wrong crowd, throwing myself into a life of stolen pride, racing cars, and drunken fights.

Amidst the chaos of my life, something strange happened in high school psychology class. During a guided visualization, I had a lucid vision of driving through a gentle rain on a beautiful summer day. The road ahead curved abruptly, and my car slid into the ditch and flipped in slow motion. I was thrown, tumbling into a forest of dead trees. I heard shattering glass and a painful scream, and then everything went black. The next moment, I was standing on the road, watching steam rise from the wreckage of my car, which lay upturned among splintered wood and scattered shrubs. The hazy figure of a man appeared overlooking my dead body. Gary? I moved closer. No, this man was much older and had a mustache. He turned toward me, and my eyes were locked in his penetrating gaze.

The experience was hauntingly real. I didn't know who the man was, but his face was strangely familiar. Was it a premonition? Was I going to die? I knew my life was out of control, and though I wanted to change, I felt powerless to do so.

My drinking turned to drugs, and as a lost soul without a prayer, I spiraled down in self-destruction.

One night after a jealous fistfight with another boy over the loss of my girlfriend, I found myself in jail. In the windowless cell, I sat on the edge of the cold steel bed frame with my head bent down, staring at the sewer in the center of the floor.

I was tripping my brains out on LSD.

The whole cell started rocking like a ship in the grip of a cyclone. I closed my eyes to escape, but my inner world was a whirlpool sucking me into a dark abyss.

A shooting pain in my stomach buckled me over onto the floor. I dragged myself to the toilet and heaved convulsively. Completely exhausted, I collapsed back to the floor and stared upward. As I began a slow descent into unconsciousness, the silhouette of the man with the mustache stood over me, surrounded by a strange light.

"Who are you? What do you want?" I whispered. Every cell in my body tingled.

A voice that sounded far away replied,

Come to me.

At that moment, I felt my soul being pulled out through the top of my head. Fading into a bright light, I thought I was dying as I began to pass out.

The sound of heavy keys clanking in the cell lock woke me. The cage door swung open, and an officer ordered, "Get up. Your parents are here."

I peeled myself off the concrete floor and tried to stand, but my head was spinning. Losing my balance, I braced myself against the wall but fell on the bed frame. My right hand was swollen and bloody with cuts across the knuckles. My clothes were filthy, speckled with dried vomit. I hesitated with the dread of facing my parents looking like this.

Finally I stood up, brushed myself off, and followed the officer into the waiting room. My mother gasped when she saw me. My father put his arm around her and said coldly, "Come on, son. Let's go home."

On the way back, he cursed angrily under his breath and asked, "What the hell are you doing with your life?"

I hung my head in shame and said nothing.

When we got home I cleaned up, went straight to my room, and shut the door. My head was throbbing, my throat was raw, and every muscle in my body ached. I flopped on my bed face down and buried myself in the corner where the mattress met the wall to hide myself from daylight.

Hours later, Mom came in and sat by my side with her hand on my back. "Dinner's ready." Her hand nervously clawed at my shoulder. I turned slightly and saw that the sunset had colored my room orange. I didn't answer. "You know, it's not too late," she said. "You can turn your life around. Isn't it time you learned the difference between right and wrong?"

She patted my hair like she used to when I was a child. "Right or wrong, it's your choice, dear," she whispered. "It's not too late." She didn't understand. With Gary gone, I didn't care about my life.

Mom sighed and got up. I heard her shuffle through the books on my shelf. She sat back down and read aloud to me but I couldn't hear her above the wailing trumpets in my head. She stopped reading, sat quietly for a few minutes, and left.

As I turned over to watch the fading sunlight, the book she was reading fell on the floor. As the cover came into focus, I thought I was hallucinating. There was the man with the mustache, the man from my roadside vision, the same man I saw in jail. I flipped it open and read:

... could you keep your heart in wonder at the daily miracles of your life, your pain would not seem less wondrous than your joy.

I closed the book and looked at the drawing of the man with the mustache again, puzzled. Something unfamiliar crawled up my spine, and my whole body tingled with pins and needles. I sat up, but I was too confused to make sense out of anything. I opened the book at random again, and my eyes fell on another line:

. . . even as love crowns you so shall he crucify you.

These words fell on my ears and struck a cord deep in the quiet of my heart. With the book in hand, I walked into the kitchen.

"Mom, who is this?"

"That's your great uncle Kahlil. You should read his book; it's beautiful," she said.

I put some dinner on a plate and went to my room with *The Prophet*.

Shutting the door behind me, I flipped through the pages, reading lines at random until it was dark. The wind was howling outside. A bright flash of lightning was followed by a loud thunderclap that shook the house, and then the rain came pouring down.

I watched the rain build up at the top of the window and stream down over the panes. My eyes swelled, and with rhythmic convulsions, I let go of the storm within me.

For the first time since Gary's death, I cried my heart open.

As I cried, I prayed; I prayed to Gary, to God, and to the mysterious man with the mustache. A mystical light filled the room, and what happened thereafter would change me forever.

From that moment on, I never stopped praying. I prayed on mountain tops, in the dark when I was lost, and with the dawn of each new day.

This book is part of the story of how my prayers were answered through a series of prophetic episodes that revealed the hidden purpose of my life.

Yesterday, between dawn and twilight, I was forever attempting to make sense of the mystery of existence. I thought my lifetime a mere flicker of the flame of eternity, a tenuous speck of dust lifted momentarily by the sentient winds that roam through the infinite sphere.

Today, I am enchanted by the direct experience of an invisible presence that somehow knows my needs better than I wanted to admit.

For many years an inner prompting beckoned me to rise to my spiritual calling, but I doubted the truth I was destined to realize, and in my doubt, I suffered. I was a wounded man dreaming of love yet not ready to be the one I prayed to become.

Now the dream has grown to shape the very core of my life and shake the foundation of who I know myself to be.

While I was unaware of my expansion and bemoaning the confusion of my emergence, a joy sweeter than music and greater than laughter came to me. The one who prayed was pulled inward by the sheer immensity of the one who answered.

Eventually, my spiritual quest took me to my great uncle's tomb high in the mountains of Lebanon. As I sat in silence in the monastery where Kahlil's body rests, I was overcome with feelings of homecoming, and afterwards, I was instinctually led through the nearby village of Bsharri to find inexplicable evidence of my previous life there.

Later, intent on writing an account of my bewildering experiences, my hand was guided by the unseen, yet now familiar, presence. I witnessed the words emerge effortlessly from my deepest feelings, but in a dialect not my own. Even now I sit spellbound as my pen glides with the ease of an angel's grace.

Much of what is conveyed to me comes as profound, yet subtle impressions. I am in awe to witness on these pages the thoughts that express the epiphanies of my heart.

I share my story with you because I believe it is your story too. The prophet represents the spirit that dwells in all of us. I pray that my book helps us awaken to our common spirituality. Together in love we are divine.

With great joy I offer you this parable of spiritual awakening based on my journey into the light. May it ignite a celebration of love in your heart.

DAWN

From a sleepless dream within the immense sea of silence, love's grace gathered dust and dew for a dwelling place in another body. The towers of yesteryears faded into a sealed memory and were forgotten in the resurrection of my innocence.

I was reborn in the twilight shadows of a world at war with itself. I knew not that the stage was set for the awakening of a new dawn after a dark night of human drama, for I was one with the world where life is forever young and the day is immaculate and new. My heart was a joy wanting to sing and a river ready to flood.

My parents in their love said, though I was born of their flesh, my soul was conceived from life's eternal longing.

There were many who loved me, who spoke of a light they beheld in my eyes. But being merely

1

half awake, my innocence became entangled in a labyrinth of fears and desires. As the hours, days, and weeks burned through my youth, I wrestled with my shadow.

I struggled inwardly to find peace amid the harsh realities of the world. My soul echoed the incessant cry I felt in the soul of humanity.

From poor, aggrieved multitudes suffering under the heavy foot of the stonehearted;

From countless dispossessed children lost and forgotten on crowded roads to nowhere;

From the hollow babble of hypocritical warlords who assault with pious vengeance, maiming the innocent, leaving the war-torn wailing with terror;

Nightmares reared their hooves in blackened skies over my cowering fears of worse times to come.

In distrust of unjust authority figures, I closed my heart to a Higher Power. The negation in my soul stood as a dark ghost obscuring my inner light, and I suffered in silent knowledge of my lost joy.

I hungered for love and thirsted for wisdom. I yearned for freedom and the power to stand in the glory of a higher destiny. Like the force trapped within a seedstone, I needed to break through the dark encasement of my unconsciousness.

As my youth drew to a close, my heartache grew more immediate.

From birth I basked in the warmth of my older brother's love. On the tragic day he died, I fell deep into a dark abyss.

In a reservoir of repressed tears, damned by fears, I spiraled down into a dark underworld—

Undone—

Unsung.

Without hope, I choked against the weight of sorrow in my writhing belly of imploded emotions. The muted agony within me fought violently against tormenting trumpets of rage, terror, and anguish.

I wore my pain like a dirty trench cloak through dungeons of denial. No window to beauty in that hellhole, only a drain to a sewer in the center of the floor through which I descended. I plummeted down a dour abyss of misery, with nowhere to turn but around.

Unable to bear this grief, the final threads of my fragile strength severed, and the floodgates opened.

Drowning in a tsunami of emotion, I cried out in prayer to the guardian of my soul:

"Help me, please. Wrap your comfort around me, lift me from this misery, and carry me in your embrace. Bathe me in your light, and let me rest in your love."

Through my tear-blurred vision, a brilliant radiance permeated the room and enveloped me in warmth. Mesmerized, I turned toward the light and heard the gentle whisper of an angel's voice:

The well of love that waters your garden is at times filled with your tears.

And it is good that it is so, for no waters are purer than those precious droplets released in your moments of surrender.

Tears are seed drops of joy shed by your soul's physician.

You may curse the physician's medicine, but the cure for your suffering is in your tears.

Weep until seeds of joy take root in the womb of your soul.

Bless grief, as it softens the sinew that shields your deprived heart. Yield to pain, for armor must be torn from you to expose your innocent strength.

I would have you find innocence with joy rather than pain. But what joy is there that knows not pain? Verily, pain is your necessity. As your needs subside, joy will lift you with pure delight to your home in love.

Be patient, for time has a way of putting wings on tears.

Your pain is your need for love. I am the love you need.

Drink the vital elixir from my well-spring that one day your heart may become a fountain where all whose dreams of love have died may drink.

Wiping my eyes with astonishment and squinting into the blinding light, I saw a dreamy figure of a man standing before me. Startled, I spoke defensively:

"My heart is torn, and I am drowning in sorrow. Who are you to speak of love in my time of grief?"

The messenger of love answered:

Though I am called by many names, I am nameless and formless, yet I appear to you always in a form that draws you to me.

I am the spirit pulsing in the heart of all beings.

Like the seed of the fruit, I hold the secrets of life from before the dawn of creation.

Your pain is the cracking of the seed that contains your larger self.

In conflict you stretch the limits of your being.

6

Just as a butterfly writhes to free itself from the confines of its chrysalis that it may fly free, your journey is a metamorphosis of the soul.

From the survival instincts of primal man, you are reborn again and again, that at last you may soar on enlightened wings of love.

I am with you through aeons of rebirth just as you are with the seasons of your sentience.

As the blurred apparition became more defined, I sensed the presence of my brother but in the shape of an older man I knew only in my dreams. He continued:

I have come to guide you through this night of anguish that you might glimpse beyond the haze of your clouded mind and troubled heart.

Though your brother has vanished, his spirit lives on, forever bonded with the timeless.

The love you share with him is safe from the shifting tides of time and form.

You and he abide together in an unseen realm where you both know what it is not yours to know here.

And just as you were reborn from that limitless sphere of exalted light, so shall he.

The gaping wound in your heart is the doorway to your higher destiny, yet your anguish overshadows the grandeur of the legacy bestowed upon you.

You are here to imbue the light of compassion into this world mired in matter.

Through this painful passage you will come to regard all humanity as you do your brother.

Your love for him is a small portion of the vast love that lies dormant within you.

And in this, your darkest hour, you are closest to love's entry.

When all seems lost, you are most apt to find the inconceivable treasure.

And how would you realize your brilliance but in a world that offers you less than it needs you to be?

Your light is revealed by the darkness it dispels.

BELIEF

Before the light appeared to me, I looked no further than the horizon for nourishment. Now I sought a sustenance that had no horizon.

Before spirit soothed my wound, I found comfort in the sympathy of my companions and the bosom of my family, but they were no comfort for these intangible needs.

Before the prophet spoke to me personally, I was resigned to be a pawn of destiny.

I thought God was the unknowable king on an unreachable throne, a mighty figment to whom I could pray to quench my thirst, only to kneel in silence, sipping a faint trickle of hope.

For a time, I gave my faith to religious myths told and retold through generations. I studied venerated books, prayed in churches, bowed in temples, and prostrated myself before altars. But I could not content myself with such beliefs. I needed to touch the formless substance and commune with realms that remain hidden.

In my search for faith, I met many who listened to no song unlike their own anthem. They stood proud, wearing their beliefs like suits of fine linen. I could see their naked vulnerability clinging to their tenets like a frightened child grasping her mother's dress for comfort and strength. But they hid their strength from themselves and suffered a worse sacrifice in their comfort, for their convictions muted that which is more than human in us.

In these peculiar ways, life taught me.

I learned faith from the doubter, decency from the sinister, compassion from the cruel, and gratitude from them all.

When I looked through the eyes of the most high, I saw that I was all of them. Each person added to my enchantment as each star helps illuminate the great mystery of the cosmos.

I met a precious few whose religion was a humble light that gleamed as serenely as any star in the heavens. They spoke not of ideologies; rather, they guided me to my inner sanctuary to commune with the Nameless One.

The spirit that revealed itself to me embraces all beings—believers and agnostics alike. It comes as a vast halo that permeates everyone and everything that has been, reaching always farther to encompass all that ever shall be.

In this deep sea of mystery I prayed for something to rest my faith upon with certainty. The prophet answered:

It may comfort you to take refuge in the sanctified belief of your favor, yet hasten not to describe the mystery in your likeness, nor its ways according to your interpretation.

I would have you hold your beliefs as lightly as the thoughts they consist of.

Ideologies reach out with many arms and a multitude of fingers, all extending away from the center.

Leave your religious doctrines on the shelves of history. They are a fading echo of the ancients who came long after your birth.

And you will remain long after the deified books retire into a dusty memory.

For your beginning was not in the womb, nor will you meet your end in the grave.

You will never comprehend enough to fathom the miraculous.

And you can only hope for that which you have yet to realize.

Lest you have faith, you are like a feather cast on the wind, drifting aimlessly.

Yet if your faith is confined to your convictions, you are like a caged bird that may unfold its wings but cannot fly free.

Though you may enjoy the comfort of your convictions, your psyche is prone to stagnate in confinement.

Your faith must not keep you, nor define or divide you.

Build not a refuge of your faith; rather, let it be a glistening archway to the boundless presence within you.

You are so much more magnificent than anything you can conceive, yet you are only revealed to yourself to the degree that your realization allows.

You would build of your beliefs a vessel on which to navigate the rolling sea of life; I would have you dive into fathomless depths to be one with your elemental soul.

Though you would have me be a fountain where you dip your cup in moments of thirst, I would be a flood that drowns you, for in your undoing is your unfolding.

I would erase all of your beliefs that you might come to me with more of your innocence and less of your convictions.

Though you carve my words into stone and proclaim them as reflections of truth, I turn stone into mist and melt all that is crystallized into liquid melody.

I am the ever-present song you have yet to sing; nearer to you than your breath.

You may search the world to find me, yet I can only be found within you.

For I am your heart enlightened and your mind enchanted.

TRUTH

Longing to know the depths of life's mystery, I passed my time in contemplation. On lonely walks into the night, amid the splattered moonlight beneath the shelter of the forest, I dreamt of the spirit world.

As I dreamt, the scent of a faraway wind gave hint of a revelation made more pure by my passage through darkness.

Gazing humbly into the limitless sky, I marveled to myself:

"In these vast, magnificent heavens, who am I? From where have I come and by what means do I appear here? What better purpose have I than to marvel at my predicament in the ambiguity of time?"

The starlight whispered a message from the prophet's invisible presence:

Time is the heartbeat of eternity, a soundless throb rippling through the depths of space.

Mother Ocean performs her rhythmic dance with the moon, measuring time ceaselessly. Father Mountain knows time as aeons of precipitation carve canyons into his stubborn resistance.

Ticking perpetually on a seamless sequence of moments, time is the gatekeeper to all phenomena. And none can stay the hands thereof, as all things change.

Yet suspended on glistening threads of perception, between clouded memories of having been and a forever approaching horizon, you are the still witness of all that passes before you.

Every wonderful thing vanishes, every sweet feeling fades as you remain the unseen observer.

And from your first thought, time is born.

In your search for truth, look beyond the lineal fields of time and logic.

Climbing a conceptual ladder on rungs of reasoning, you will simply arrive where you have always been.

Truth is a paradoxical abyss that you stumble upon, and there it is, smiling at you, unadorned and as irrational as love.

In the quiet of your heart you can intuit the laws that sculpt your life and shape your destiny.

Shake off your preconceived opinions. Each moment you dip your cup into the river of creation it is fresh and new.

A truth uttered dwells but a moment upon your lips. And a truth remembered is not truth; it is yesterday's reflection in the mirror of time.

Concepts cast spells upon immaculate perception, reducing the miraculous to facts.

Listen to the serenity beyond the semblance of these thoughts. Release your mind from any mirage of meaning. Let your tongue taste more than the stale breath of knowledge drawn from books of another time and place. Be a beacon of the truth that springs from the spontaneous impulse of your soul.

You are the Living Truth.

You are a ray of the Supreme Being who illuminates your world with consciousness, that you may delight in fields of dreams.

With the first wink of the sun your daydream begins: you think you are awake, but your dream goes on in the sleep of forgetfulness.

Could you remember who you are, you would laugh with the gods at the absurdity of your seriousness.

*And know that before and after all this has come
and gone—*
   There you are as I am.

DESIRE

The prophet's train of reasoning exceeded my grasp, yet his wisdom served as a balm to my inflamed feelings.

The fear and pain of my past began to part like heavy curtains only to expose a deeper yearning. My spiritual experiences teased me with their intoxicating elixir and then left me bound in mortal cravings.

One warm spring day, I lazed by a meandering brook that whirled and eddied around sharp rocks before disappearing down a narrow canyon. Watching a wild crocus slowly push its way through the earth's crust, I recognized myself—an unborn bud confined by a lingering winter. I needed the freedom of success before my heart could truly blossom.

Like casting jewels into a deep sea, I had given everything to be intimate with my spiritual calling, but the visionary experiences were dreamlike and fleeting. I was left more impoverished, for I became idle and depleted my accounts in search of incorporeal wealth.

It was not a fleeting thought I yearned for but a primordial need for tangible assets. My pockets were empty, my hands unprofitable, and I was in want of sustenance.

"Teach me of money," I asked, "for is it not by this medium that earthly success is measured and security gained?"

The babbling brook became a melody to my ears as the prophet answered:

I would have you gain mastery in all your means, but measure not your worth nor success with money, for money cannot make love and your worth is in making love visible.

Your desire for success is at the core of your failing, for only when you are empty of desire will success fill you.

A person may control nations triumphantly and be honored throughout generations, yet feel little self-worth. While another, in the simplest existence, may inspire an awakening of the soul yet be neither acknowledged nor remembered by name.

Where is worth found and from where does it come? What worth has a blade of grass next to a majestic sequoia?

Only you give yourself worth, or not.

And just as the earth yields her fruit unto you according to the seeds you sow, so too is your soul a field of abundance that the heavens shower blessed manna upon according to the dreams you seed in this formless substance.

The answers to your highest aspirations lie waiting in the untapped source within you.

If you are an opportunist in pursuit of fame and fortune, you rob yourself of your inner treasures, like a miner who forsakes nature's beauty to obtain her glittering gold.

Voracious pursuits will quench your desires as effectively as bucketing fuel upon a fire to extinguish it.

The want for more will never be enough, for that which you do not need does little to satisfy.

Let your aspirations be exalted beyond the superficial allure of soul-defeating gains.

Money can neither unchain your heart nor unveil your beauty.

It cannot guide your feet in dance nor free your voice in song.

Only your openness can fill your emptiness.

Like a blind man at a banquet table, often the hungry mouth of poverty ignores the outspread offerings of the Provider.

Prosperity begins by recognizing this magnificent world as your playground.

With the meditative seriousness of a child on a treasure hunt, find your well of inspiration, that you may offer creative solutions to the problems you perceive.

Your desire is life's desire for itself. What do you truly want but the freedom and power to love your dreams into being? What greater power can you enjoy than the freedom to love as you are?

What can tomorrow bring that is not yours now?

You are a child in the garden of grace, supported on whatever plane you choose to play.

And the greatest treasure you will ever find is in the love you share.

Consider the precious gift to be here alive—to touch, to feel, to love.

Bargain not the present for a keepsake or a promise.

GRACE

These inner dialogues penetrated my insecurity and loosened the shackles of my confinement, but I still denied myself the freedom to live in grace.

I woke each morning under the burden of my own weight, and my waking dream was overmindful of its yearning for a distant treasure.

Like a disembodied spirit desperately seeking refuge from an intangible storm, I wallowed through waves of arbitrary confusion that I could neither end nor endure.

I pleaded to the spirit of my soul:

"Your voice arouses in me a passion for the unseen.

I recognize the majesty of my world, yet still I stand before you with the ache of wanting.

The hand of a ghost is upon my throat and the taste of bitter days still burns in my belly.

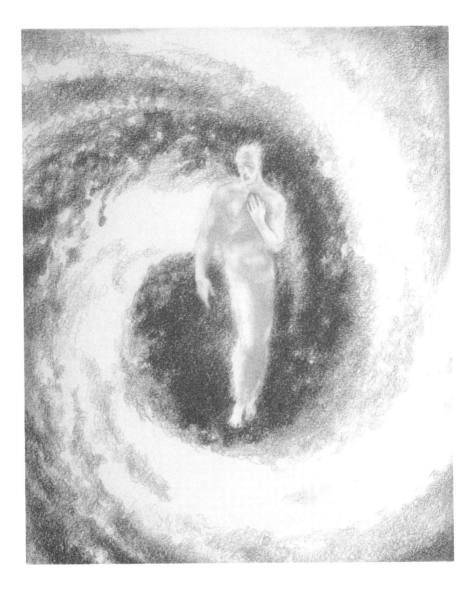

My troubled heart beats in hunger for your presence.

I long to join you in this garden of grace of which you speak, yet how shall I unless you be my all?''

After a quiet moment the prophet spoke to me tenderly:

How many ways can I weave your awakening into words that you may behold the state of grace in your thoughts?

You were born in grace's garden at the dawn of creation. Nothing more than your graciousness can be added to the depth and breadth of grace's splendor.

Ripples on a pond display the texture of a breeze just as a smile reveals the face of the spirit.

Grace speaks in soft colors and caresses your senses with benevolent whispers.

She serves up a glorious banquet and does her best to awaken you for her feast.

Grace carries you always homeward and forever would lead your feet to dance on the very ground that will claim them.

It is your privilege to star in the sacred play of light and shadow that was staged to celebrate your birth. Your innate polarity is projected into the presence of all that appears before you.

You may suffer in discord with your reflection, but prior to the shadow play, the light of spiritual grace shines eternally upon you.

Whether in peace or conflict, you meet what you bring; this recognition initiates your enlightenment. The measure of your attainment is demonstrated by your emanation of grace through scenes of adversity.

The grace you are after is before you always, but in fear of need, you deny it.

The illusion of need hangs like a veil over your eyes. To worry of want while in this garden of plenty is to cast yourself into a sequel of lack.

Loosen the knot of need and remove fear's blindfold that you may see this extravagant playhouse through the eyes of the preeminent Player.

Grace overfilled your cup long before the fear of want was conceived. Patiently she waits with delight for those precious moments when you pause to notice.

SEXUALITY

I was sailing a calm sea of dreams when waves of youthful lust swelled within me.

Love's lips whispered poetry in my ears and opened my eyes to see beauty in the shape of woman. She became the supreme vision of divine form that gave meaning to my existence.

To me, she was more exalted than the sky, deeper than the sea, and more perplexing than either, I worshiped her beauty and yearned to enter the womb of her affection.

Merging together in love became the only thing I desired. But the Creator made two bodies of one and cast them into worlds far apart where separation was agony. The slightest touch of her soft skin left my heart throbbing like the trembling mouth of a man thirsting in the desert. She was the most beautiful of all creation, and she appeared lovelier through the mist of my lustful longing.

Everything changes in accord with the emotions of the beholder; thus, my infatuation deluded my senses.

I romanticized the light of her eyes, the sweet tone of her voice, and the elegance of her figure. If I were to hold such a woman as I imagined, she would surely dissolve in my embrace.

I looked upon her like a seer who gazes into the great mystery to discover its secrets. My longing saw her as something more divine than I, and my worth diminished in my gaze, for the virtue I worshiped in her I denied in myself.

In my fantasies I was haunted by seductive visions of untamed lust. My own thoughts sent flaming arrows into my heart, for I wanted to devour the one I adored.

Through her eyes angels looked down upon the lowly in me with a look of disgust, and my chest caved in shame.

But nothing would appease my passion, for my purpose was clear, as though it were engraved in my memory at the dawn of eternity.

With my head buried in my hands, I screamed to summon my despondent spirit:

"I am haunted by an obsession that enslaves me. My heart is a wild tiger crashing against a cage of unspoken principles.

Help me untangle that which is sacred from that which is shameful in sexuality, that I may become a man worthy of a woman's love."

The prophet answered with an empathetic tone:

Of the sacred I will speak, but first let us undress the sham from the shameful.

What is shame but a cloak woven of morality, draped around the innocent?

Though you cover your nakedness with morals, you conceal much of your beauty only to protect the eyes of the impure. In doing so, you postpone your meeting with the goddess whose sight is undefiled by your naked desires.

Think not that you can direct love's course with precepts of righteousness.

And see that you do not bow before the pious, deeming it respect.

All is sacred within love's compassionate heart.

When life is tortured by its own hunger in dungeons of denial, the innocent will suckle on the breasts of demons if need be.

Who knows that a plight of indignity be not for your expansion?

For the Creator is also the Destroyer, and there are hidden blessings to be found in every haunt and on every summit along life's sacred journey.

They alone are exalted who make love with their shadow and turn the discord of their soul into a song made sweet with lessons learned.

Therefore, linger not in the swamps of lust lest you lose your way.

Come to lovemaking for more than a sensate thrill or seductive indulgence.

Though your animal-self knows its needs and will not be betrayed, so too does your god-self, who needs you tenderly ripened in love.

Sexual intimacy can propel you to the most blissful moments of true union and plunge you into the emotional underworld where you meet your unborn soul.

Together you are the many faces of the Faceless One playing all.

In half sleep you become infatuated by the spell of your wholeness passing through each other's form. Though you yearn to merge, your wholeness is realized through your virtue in relation to each other. And that which you adore in each other is for you to realize within yourself.

Your bodies are temples of spirit; when you meet for sexual communion, bring your heart's prayer to be seeded in the womb of creation. Let love's visions take sensual shape in the fervent pulse.

Utterly surrender to the Goddess that she may soften you, full, ripe, and delicious. Arch your soul up to the divine and welcome God to satiate your expansiveness.

At last, as your bodies absorb the throbbing of ecstasy, let your desires grow quiet in a heaven full of loving whispers.

CHANGE

The procession of days freed me from the bondage of solitude by leading me to a woman who filled me with joy. She invited me into the bosom of her tenderness, and I willingly entered to be tutored in her intimate secrets.

A great happiness was born in me from her affection. She enchanted me with love's melodies, filling the hours with music and turning my loneliness into bliss.

We were wed in the summer of love, and from honeymoon nights we woke each morning with a love song on our lips. Our passion blessed our home with two precious children.

Those days were like pages of a romance novel I would never finish reading, for our family was a lifespring from which I drank my happiness with pride.

Amidst the clamor of life, my heart found a resting place where I was content to witness the commotion of our world.

The months and years passed quickly, like shadows of clouds over hills and valleys, every day of which held an aeon of memories.

The sun that gives life to the garden in spring will burn it dry come summer.

A cyclone may begin with a subtle wave of butterfly wings.

Every occurrence in the story of life is first born of wistful thoughts and dreams.

I don't remember the adverse thoughts that were seeded into our happy dream. I didn't notice the ill-omened frowns amidst our busy days. And I cannot recapture the strained moments that changed our feelings.

The sea of our love pushed us steadily to the shores of two worlds far apart.

Soon little of our love remained, save distant memories of our marriage flapping like tattered flags in the aftermath of a storm.

Our love died in a squall that struck with flashes of lightning and thunderous truths, leaving all of our faces drenched in tears.

One evening in late autumn, I lay shaken by the tempest that destroyed our family and left me a father isolated from his children.

My throat was choked with grief, and I writhed in agony to release the sobs that were imprisoned in my chest.

My eyes, which used to marvel at the wonders of nature, saw only a barren landscape laid waste by the storm's fury.

My ears, which used to delight in the laughter of children, heard only an echo of the howling winds of wrath.

I, who once rejoiced in the bond of family, was now tortured by the disappointing saga of love's failure.

Nothing was more precious to me than those warm days of love, and nothing was more heartbreaking than these horrid nights of cold despair.

I had hoped to make something extraordinary of my life. Now, weak and wounded, I sought a cave where the world would cease to exist, where my name would be rubbed out from the memory of time.

But the more I sought darkness, the brighter was my soul shining tenderly upon me.

Often, by mysterious means, the prophet entered my melancholy as a vague image or fleeting

sensation, and other times, he appeared as a glow-
ing phantom in the sky.

One evening I spoke to him in earnest:

"In this dark hour the burden of love's loss beats
heavy on my heart.

I pray for the rebirth of joy out of yesterday's
pain.

I long to bask in the tranquility of a day renewed
by the grace of forgetfulness.

I beg for the wisdom to abide with integrity and
the passion to celebrate virtue.

But I am disheartened by my failure to live up to
even my most modest expectations.

I wish your mercy could release my weakness
that my strength could walk in your light.

But how can I find consolation in your wisdom,
however rich it may be? I am like the yellow leaves
of autumn that have no use for the sun's golden
rays. They are but playthings for the wind that
makes way for the howling cry of winter."

The prophet's mighty presence appeared before
me like a lofty mountain, unshaken by my quak-
ing soul. He answered in a way that disclosed no
pity:

As you drink the bitter wine of winter today,

forget not that the songs of spring sleep on the lips of tomorrow.

Your grief is a dark cloud eclipsing the luster of your mind, raining tears upon your heart that the tree of life may blossom again.

The turbulent emotions that pass through your heart follow the same laws that direct the rivers toward the deep.

Surrender as a river surrenders to its source; you will be lifted above the hills again and again, until at last you descend, laughing through the valleys on your way home.

I come not to comfort but to shake your roots in their clinging to the underworld that you might shed your sorrowful thoughts and lift your head above the clouds of limited thinking.

The lesser one within you complains over life's failure to oblige your burdens.

You suffer as a testament to the truth of your grievance.

And your misery endures as you wrestle with your ghoul through the chasm where birth's agony echoes off the walls of death's impending presence.

With your back to the light you are bound to grow weary in the insipid shadow you yourself cast.

More than the fragile one you think you are, I applaud that which is formless and free within you.

Your soul is of boundless depth, and your spirit frolics through the great beyond.

Why show me only an odious morsel of your giant self?

Call upon your depth to rise unto your height that you may summit the mountains of your remaining days as stepping-stones to the zenith in your soul.

What passionate strength will lift your head with dignity in the midst of your suffering?

What power will move you to sing, even as you cry for help, or dance, even as you beg for mercy?

You are a dreamer in the making.

What inspired vision will make you fearless in your world and lead you into the glory of your enlightened heart?

VISION

Embittered with grief, I continued to complain:

"I am enslaved by laws I don't understand, and my burden bends my head to see the shattered fragments of my life on the ground.

You would have me turn devoutly to the heavens again, but I am a withered flower choked by thistles and thorns. I bid my beauty farewell.

I am lost in an unending storm of broken dreams with only moans of regret ringing in my ears, and you would have me drift further into a fanciful haven of visions.

But my lamp is dim, and I strain to read what is written on the ashen face of these ungrateful days.

My prayers are the prayers of love's fool in doubt, and it seems you believe in me more than I do myself."

The prophet answered:

The words you utter in prayer are inconsequential to the words, thoughts, and images upheld through the hours of your days.

Your path will forever follow your imaginings as surely as your days follow your nights.

The life you meet is an inescapable reflection of how you look at it.

Everything begins and ends as a dream. Your personal saga is but a daydream before the dawn of your larger self. Yesterday your vision sought wisdom, but today your wisdom must seek higher vision.

Open the windows and doors in your loft. Let a fresh wind blow away the rubble that clutters your psyche.

Unbolt the secret cupboards in your imagination and feed your hungry heart with blessed manna.

Visions come from a secret force you have yet to discover, and they lead you onward into the periphery of promise.

To dream is to commune with the vast and to touch that which is forever out of reach.

Your healing dream exposes a secret pathway to an enchanted world.

It is your place to spark the light of enchantment to shine from behind your eyes.

Always do your best to reveal your brilliance.

With patience, endure your bleaker days.

For the best in you scores highest in failed attempts.

And it is your brilliance that transforms today's failure into the victories of tomorrow.

Beyond your reach, tomorrow is forever a promise away. You'll never moor in her port, but she casts her spell upon your day. She holds all that is possible. She is the treasure keeper's purpose, the traveler's destiny.

After all, are you not but a voyager in time, riding on waves of change?

You are the captain of the vessel of your mind floating through consciousness.

Without imagination your mind is as futile as a boat without the sea.

Your visions of tomorrow set the sails on your course.

To sail on the breeze of your most noble aspirations is to arrive at your supreme destination.

Only then will you be the one you pray to become.

Now will you emerge from your self-pity with the wit to dream yourself into being indomitable?

ABUNDANCE

The power of the prophet's wisdom began to penetrate my understanding, and the doors of tomorrow opened by invisible means as I walked toward my destiny with his voice reverberating within me.

Visions flooded my solitude like waves from unknown seas crashing on the shores of my soul.

By night I received messages not meant for my days. Often I woke with prophetic dreams that had burned their way through to my memory, as if some intelligent light from a distant star was seeking a haven in my heart.

Though I was unable to fully voice these love songs passing on the wind, their taste was upon my tongue, and they left a smile upon my lips.

When I did speak, the faint echo of their murmur could be heard beneath my breath. In this way, I became known as one who communes with spirits of another world, and soon I was looked upon as a spiritual teacher and healer.

For many years I went wherever I was invited, traveling from place to place, offering healing, and teaching the ways of love and spiritual awakening.

Eventually I found my home in Hawaii, where people were quick to accredit me with mystical powers. Some said I lived in their sleepless memory, visiting them with messages in the night. Several were of affluent means, and as they prospered, they rewarded me generously.

My pockets overfilled with abundance and my investments multiplied. I acquired a sizable fortune that included a beautiful estate where I began to build a spiritual retreat center with an ever-expanding vision for the future.

As my wealth grew, so did a puffed up feeling of self-importance.

The more I was offered, the more I wanted; the more I was given, the more I needed.

I endured a flawed version of the man I aspired to be. A hollow chill made me mindful of my pride feeding on my followers. I longed for the warmth of an unpretentious life.

When at last I gazed into the mirror, the penetrating presence of the prophet reflected back at me.

His words of wisdom found their way to my weakness:

You came into this world with fists clenched with the purpose of opening.

Your emptiness would have you fill your life with substance, but you know little of the source that will satisfy your discontentment, so you cling to things in compensation for your spiritual poverty.

As your fate unfolds, your dominion grows in kind. All things are added unto you according to your maturity. But nothing is for your keeping, for you belong not to the world of things. Thus, seek not artificial wealth, for only a fountain in your heart can satisfy your thirst.

Prosperity is a fickle friend who can rob you of your virtue. And you are never so vulnerable as in times when the streams of affluence and fame overflow your wishing well.

Beware the effects of good fortune, for that which you possess possesses you and so has the power to destroy you.

Under the burden of excess, your innocence is too easily crippled with pride.

And as you amass assets, you amass anxiety in proportion. Thus, you rise with success and fall in misfortune according to your attachments.

In this muck you must build the foundation of your character, but nothing so belittles your character as an obsession with wealth or the desire to be admired.

To seek a higher life by enhancing anything above your heart's disposition is a futile endeavor.

Think not that only the sun-bathed peaks of prosperity are worthy of your favor, for rare blessings appear as well in unadorned deserts.

Virtue is a modest friend who would lead you empty-handed through sequestered valleys to a lifespring of simple joys.

If you snub the virtuous life in pursuit of extravagance, your journey will beget trouble at every step.

For just as pouring ink into your well taints it black, pure pleasure is polluted by desire. But, at last, nothing is so foul that a touch of innocence cannot make it pure again.

Prosperity need not hinder your progress, nor can renunciation elevate your goodness.

It is your weakness that worships wealth, and so must you exercise your strength to serve a greater good.

In truth, it is life that serves you as an honored guest in this elusive palace of time. Only a fool would try to hoard the intangible whispering of the hours, while through a generous heart, the drone of days turns to sweet music.

Give that you may know the joy of giving, for when your time is done all that you have not given will be lost.

Through the bounty of your kindness the pauper in you is christened a prince.

Generosity is your crowning jewel, well worth the cost of a hundred million desires.

BETRAYAL

I mouthed these principles to enhance my value in the eyes of others, but I was not ready to live up to them. Nor was I ready to be the captain of my ship on the rising seas of abundance. I doubted my ability to manage my growing assets, and in my doubt, I was tossed between fear of loss and desire for more. I could hear the voice of wisdom, but I was bound by glittering chains of attachment.

I needed help.

Of the many people who gathered around me as a family of friends, one man's true character was unknown to me. I believed his charm, kindness, and generous gestures. His voice was like a gentle rain in the desert. Often we sat together to share a meal, spiced with stories and jokes, and we laughed together with all the fullness of our hearts.

When my load was heavy he helped carry my burden as a true friend would. More than once during the years I knew him, my tears fell upon his shoulder as he held me like the brother I longed for.

I opened my heart and my home to him, but my psychic eyes remained closed.

I ignored the distance in his eyes and the unshed tears upon his face. I did not intuit the wound in his heart that kept him in a world far apart. I failed to notice that when we embraced, his hands were searching for a way into my pockets. And while we laughed together, his eyes were scanning my home with a scheme.

Behind a mask, he walked proud among the innocent, like a wolf stalking its prey. He was a thief who seduced the charitable with the cunning of a spider weaving its web, and I learned too late that many had been caught in his carefully constructed net of deceit.

He claimed that life's luxuries effortlessly followed his proficient ways of managing money, and I made the mistake of accepting his offer to manage mine.

After a decade of pouring hours into my dream and watching its beauty begin to unfold, it died.

I lost the better part of everything to deception, clever trickery, and futile lawsuits.

The blow hit hard.

Cold flames of rage erupted from my depths and leapt into the firmament, only to leave ashes in my hearth.

I went to the ocean and flayed wild fists against the battalion of waves until hopeless sorrow left me trembling on the shore among the froth.

I cried to my soul:

"You nurture me with love; now why, with lies, do you ruin me?

You kiss me with generosity and then assault me with cruelty.

You guide me with wisdom to fields of abundance and then entrap me with insurmountable obstacles.

Indeed, I am tutored with challenge and purified with tears, but in this pain, I am left withered and spent.

With your right hand, you lift me up, and with your left hand, you strike me down, yet I know not why.

You are almighty, and I am your feeble servant. Why are you destroying me?

I grow weary of this sorrowful struggle, and I lose faith in your justice, lest you show me the merit in those who betray my trust and abuse my innocence."

The prophet's mighty voice spoke firmly to my cynical heart:

You are not absolved of the wrong that is done unto you. When at last you see clearly, you will realize that the crimes committed upon you are committed for you.

Your enemy is your disowned self, whom you are too ashamed to forgive.

Gaze into your depths and you shall see his face reflected on your still waters.

Listen in the silent night, and you will feel his longing in the throbbing of your heart.

To recognize your soul in the heart of your enemy—this is the birth of true love.

Yet much of you remains unborn, concealed behind the shadows of denial.

Is it not astonishing, the power bestowed on a harmless shadow when looked upon with fear?

Opposing your enemy, you render him dangerous.

And with vengeance to punish, your own flesh is poisoned.

Any part of your world you refuse to love will turn hostile against you and thus rob you of your wholeness.

If you would ascend, you must accept all that life takes from you with the same wonder that enjoys her favors.

It is impossible to overvalue those whom you look down upon, for they offer priceless lessons.

What greater deed can one do for another than play the villain that they may give the most precious gift?

You recognize an offender's worth when you empathize with him.

Be unto him as you would have him be unto you, for through his disgrace, you have the privilege to break the chain of wrongdoings.

However, in weakness, you accuse another of what you do not accept in yourself, and you pay the price of your denial through the pain of his deeds.

Secretly, you abhor your hypocrisy and feel remorse for the grief your defiance causes.

So deftly you invited a charlatan into your home that you may recognize your worth as it bleeds in his presence.

This is your wake-up call: on the eve of your waking you must welcome your foe as your friend, for only together shall you ascend.

Your antagonist holds up a revealing mirror that reflects elusive keys to your ascension.

But spiritual liberation is not for the frail.

You must open your heart to the truth that pierces you the deepest.

FORGIVENESS

The prophet's calm presence pulled me inward like a serene lake that attracts a turbulent stream into the silent deep.

He asked me to assume responsibility for my failings and to examine myself in the mirror of my judgments.

But I battled my soul; stubborn and angry, I fought against its relentless current of wisdom.

In a fuming turmoil, I rode surging waves of noxious emotion while yearning, ironically, for the humility to be delivered into peaceful waters.

Like one searching blindly for a concealed passage from a dark prison, I prayed to understand and release my anger.

Again, the prophet answered my request:

Anger is disintegrated love.

Integrity demands that you release the element of blame that validates anger, lest you perpetuate the toxic consequence you suffer.

Flaunting in anger you make a mockery of yourself by justifying in yourself the faults you deplore in others.

Your self-righteous superiority erects a fortress of protection that becomes your prison.

Have you not yet endured enough pain in conflict?

Only a feeble heart seeks vengeance; it is the nobility of the innocent to pardon.

And your innocence is never so endearing as when praying for forgiveness.

Courageously pull back your projections and focus inward with penetrating honesty.

Break through your walls of denial and reclaim the privilege to love unconditionally.

Your wings of freedom hang in wait at the gates of heaven.

But you can enter heaven only when you love hell no less.

Unfasten the secret closets where guilt hides, and admit mercy's benevolent light.

Turn not away from shame, for it is the final veil that conceals your innate innocence.

Pour the cool waters of redemption onto the inferno that cooks up your nightmares.

Free your demons and console them on your bosom of empathy, lest they seethe in your recesses and give birth to a curse.

Much of your suffering is caused by that which you proclaim, yet your saga is but a fable upheld like a kite upon the winds of your breath.

Would that you could change your mind as freely as the wind.

For while you wallow in complaint, Beauty kisses you awake each morning with a new day. With eternal patience she whispers, "Release your burden, come outside yourself, and be with me."

And though you may turn away with little notice, she concedes always with kindness and is never offended.

COURAGE

Whispered from a world unknown, the prophet's words of wisdom were like thunder in my ears but slow to take form in my life.

My joy faded like a love song half forgotten.

My spirit left to soar somewhere between heaven and earth, leaving me but a mere shadow upon the ground.

I felt like a muddy puddle in the footprint of my soul that reflected the dream of a far distant dawn.

The sun had set in my eyes, and I knew I could reach that dawn only by way of the night.

I commiserated to myself:

"This fearful void inside me is too ungrateful to forgive.

Who does it serve to prolong this misery? I am an unwanted weight upon those around me. Out of kindness, I would leave them to join the strange dark comfort I have wished for all my life.

Brooding over my fears won't breed the courage I need. Let me confront the ultimate fear—death— that my glory not delay and follow me to my grave. Then perhaps I can sing my freedom song from the mountaintop of courage."

So I left the world of broken promises on a vision quest through the bowels of a remote canyon that extended from the island's deep interior out to the sea.

Carelessly welcoming death as twilight approached, I consumed a profusion of gold-capped mushrooms which ornamented the trail, not realizing their potency.

The moon rose in full glory and cast a nocturnal rainbow over my path, like the archway to an enchanted kingdom.

An owl guided me through the shadows that draped themselves elegantly over the canyon floor. When lost from my sight, it gave out a hoot and in this way delivered me to a circle of stones in the dark heart of the gorge.

An eerie sorcery agitated my nerves, and my sharpness of mind was blunted by the psychedelic frenzy feeding on my brain cells. My dizzy, weakened body was pulled by gravity's arms to lie on the earth and gaze into the lunar eye hovering in the iridescent sky.

While my body dissolved into light, the imagination of my spirit quickly awoke.

I saw a man lying alone on his deathbed. He moaned painfully, and I heard a voice saying:

Come, I will show you something to appease your fear. Come close, look behind the veils of death into the heart of life.

I looked upon him as the sky looks down upon the earth. And when I bent near, I beheld a contorted image of myself with grotesque features. My face was a scowl of devious wisdom, seductive tenderness, and evil beauty. The sight sent a wave of terror through my bones.

The sky became a dome of fire, consuming everything in its furious blaze. I felt my skin bubble with burning blisters. From the inside, worms gnawing at my flesh made my spirit turn pale. My quivering lips whimpered a piteous moan for mercy.

Then, like a cannon, a bolt of light shot up from my coccyx, through my spine, and exploded in my skull. An agonizing howl that could have melted a heart of stone rose from my belly and echoed out into the far reaches of the heavens.

I felt the cold affection of death too near for comfort. The door of my existence closed on its hinges, and at once, I was sure I had overdosed on poison and was dying.

Frozen with fear, I gasped one last breath while the clamoring of my heart faded into nothingness.

My spirit loosened its grip on my body as I passed through a vortex of light into a realm of radiant tranquility where I would have remained happily for eternity.

After a timeless interlude a violent quaking shook me, and my spirit was thrust back into my body.

I awoke in a pool of steaming sweat mixed with cold night dew.

My shaken interior was echoed by the faint rumble of Mount Kilauea burning a red glow on the horizon.

In my stupor, a soft blanket of fog rolled down over the canyon cliffs, and the surrounding ambiance turned ghostly calm.

After a short while, I looked around and noticed the owl perched on a large upright stone a short distance in front of me, half hidden in the haze. The owl and the stone transmuted into an apparition of the prophet.

Moving quickly toward me, he looked into my eyes and touched my forehead with his fingertips, which transmitted a message purer than any language uttered through lips.

In an instant I was in a pristine place beyond time where my mind's eye became exquisitely attuned. Mesmerized by the beauty, I felt the goodness that had previously been concealed by the horrific hallucination.

Amid silent epiphanies, my fears stood like ghosts between my gaze and the loving depths of his eyes.

And the rhythm of my heartbeat subsided into the silent beauty of his love that brought us together.

The prophet spoke, and his voice made the moonlight shimmer through the mist:

What words yet unspoken from my heart will provoke your passion song?

You've witnessed the beauty that waits beyond death, and it is good that you remember this sight.

Might you awaken enough now to realize you are dreaming, or will fear eat you alive until you are nothing but breath carried away on the wind?

I would gladly take you under my protection and bid your weakness lean on my strength, but only your courage can carry you.

You flounder on a razor's edge between the frail one you think you are and the faceless, unbound spirit that terrifies you.

But the seat of fear is in the sinister shadows of your mind.

In wakefulness, you will realize that fear itself evokes the face of that which is feared.

A chain of notions locks you into your limited identity.

And though it frightens you to dissolve into self-lessness, the emptiness you fear holds more beauty than you can imagine.

You dread not the day's end as you surrender into oblivion at night, for a new day awaits.

Beyond the clouds of forgetfulness, life shines ceaselessly through the days and nights of eternity.

And behind the scenes in your theater of despair, your essential being remains in a state of bliss.

Considering yourself so vulnerable that you become a stranger unto life's passionate play is the only tangible death.

If you hesitate to stand, afraid that the breath of life will blow out your small flame, then all will pass while you sit backstage.

Unmet fear blinds you to more noble pursuits and leads you away into superficial distractions.

And in the end, you are left with what you settle for.

Therefore, face your worst fears at once, lest you live in constant dread of them to come.

You are as safe as you can and will ever be, my child, for you are pure spirit—deathless.

Your self-image is but a sand castle built each day on the shores of time.

The tides of change are forever carrying away your most cherished creations to make way for the fresh dream being born even now.

I would have you greet your losses with wonderment and surrender your work as an offering to the giving tides.

As with all living things, you are here to realize your fullness.

Wait not for death to give birth to the vast spirit within you.

You will, in your season, return to the unremembered home of your sleepless Mother.

But death changes nothing more than the flesh that embellishes your face.

Let your days here be for living, for the white angel is ever-patient with kindness and knows better than you the moment of your readiness.

Be it a day, a decade, or an aeon from now, leave your body with a legacy of courage to all who follow behind you that you may join the triumphant ones in joyous celebration.

BLISS

The nearness to death renewed my spirit, and the storm in my heart grew quiet.

After the episode in the canyon, a tainted film was peeled from my eyes, and my world shimmered with newfound radiance.

Again the prophet's guidance unlocked my prison door and led me into fields of joy.

I was no longer held down by chains of judgment, for his wisdom taught me to appreciate that which offended me.

Now I saw only the countenance of my two selves: the one I imagined I was and the reflection of the one being born.

I applauded the prophet's mystifying presence:

"You freed me from the bondage of ignorance, and today I see clearly and walk upright, laughing with the sun. My eyes have opened from a deep

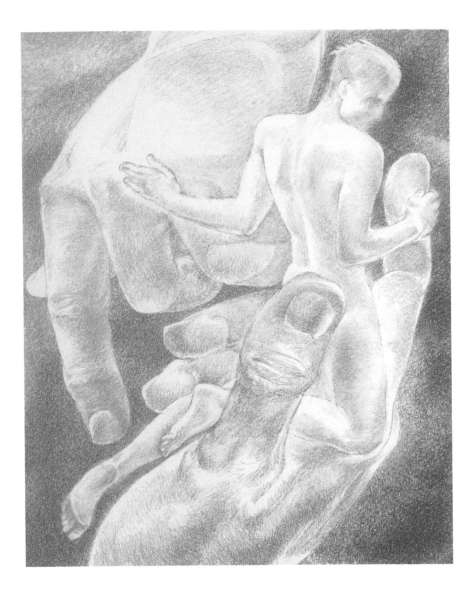

sleep, and I am at home in paradise on this day that encompasses all days.

But the keys to this mansion remain elusive, and I fear my foundation is made of clay.

You, my soul, are great by virtue of your etheric nature, but I am fickle by fault of my blind impulse. Too often I leave the overflowing fountain of the present for the appeal of nectars not yet tasted. And if I overlook my blessings one day, I am prone to overlook them the next.

I would stop this impetuous succession, but although my will is fueled with the best intentions, moles of habit burrowing in the ground undermine my footsteps. Often I stumble on the threshold between my lofty pursuit and the inertia of past patterns.

Teach me to discern your lessons that I may always follow my bliss."

The prophet answered with endearing patience:

Bliss comes to the grateful heart illuminated with presence.

Fling your gratitude far and wide along the path of your ascension.

To enjoy the harvest of your thanksgiving, you must simply cherish all that is offered upon your path from the bountiful Giver.

Should the sun cease to rise, you would see how clouded your mind becomes to the treasures lavished upon you daily.

Too often life's precious moments are not appreciated until they are lost in passing.

And though it weighs heavy upon you, forget not that half of what is given is a bitter potion prepared for your enhancement. And you could not obtain your reward in a more suiting way.

Of the dual facets of all things, one blesses you through its appearance, the other through the lessons it offers.

But often you begrudge the unwanted gifts from the shadow god, and with pride, you close your heart against that which displeases you.

Know this: you cannot find bliss if the person you choose to be is less than that which you perceive in me.

Nor can you rejoice in love if the one you think you are is greater than that which you perceive in one another.

Closed doors and erected walls block your happiness and leave you to wait unheeded in the seasonless world outside the great multiversity of life.

Even compassionate ones might pray that the world be better for the sake of their good-will.

But this I say in truth: there can be no relevant change but within the heart of the beholder.

For all that has been and ever shall be is the view you hold of it.

Everything is given unto you, save the grateful heart that would receive it.

This waits upon your willingness, which is to exercise your most exalted gift.

Until you embrace all that is with gratitude, you remain half made in the masterful hands of the Maker.

The face of life that you judge to be other than you would have it be is the symptom of your unrealized self, who alone possesses the heart to appreciate the unclaimed gifts.

Realize this key and the secret treasure that it unlocks, and all other riches will be but a penny in your pocket.

Though you might be pleased with the reward that fulfills your wish, it is a small token next to the endowment that fulfills your soul.

For then the walls come down and the gates of your heart are flung wide. And the burden you bore as a weighted chain upon your freedom adds authenticity to your joy.

With endless gratitude from one quintessential moment of awakening, an irresistible light shines upon the world through your presence.

All that can be said comes to this and nothing more, yet so much more in the full gratitude of your awakening.

Now surrender and simply savor what is offered.

LOVE

I sang out in praise:
"You come from an unimagined world and bewilder me with your brilliance.

I worship your presence within me, and in this blissful moment, I realize that I am within you.

A great joy flows as a healing elixir upon my yesterdays.

I become humbly unrecognizable to myself in your presence, for you cast a spell that charms me with your incantations.

When I listen to your soft whisper, I understand why birds sing their chorus of song to the unveiling dawn and why bees gather sweet nectar from flowers to build their home.

I give my heart as your home, to forever sing with nostalgia from your sweet music. Now please," I asked, "speak to me of love."

Have I spoken of aught else?

From love you emerge and to love you return like a raindrop falling into a ceaselessly turning sea.

The seeds of love's eternal dream were planted in you when your dream was born.

For this, your roots build a body upon the sacred earth that your rare face may be kissed by the morning dew;

That your eager arms may reach wide to gather the golden rays that warm your heart and brighten your smile;

That one day you may stand tall like a tree laden with the seeds of your loving.

Like rain and seeds, your love must be born again and again to be free.

Though you exist for each other in love, the essence of love is freedom.

Therefore, let your love be free of obligation.

Expect not another to fill your need nor follow your truth.

Nor must you follow another, for in sovereignty you discover love's deeper truth that you follow unknowingly.

Let each of you sing your own song, for the heart lends not its melody to another.

And forget not that your heart may rejoice in love alone.

If there is something you require from another for love's sake, then you stand with your head in clouds that obscure love's light.

Often you have cast shadows over yourself with outstretched hands of doubt and denial. In denying love's passion, you deny life's deeper longing for itself, wherein lies the embryo of love's most potent possibilities.

Love speaks often with gentle whispers of kindness.

And at times, love tears through the trivial with bold hands of truth.

I would that you know love as your larger self and not merely as the answer to your needs.

For love is your soul and your need.

And when you give yourself to love, you, in turn, fulfill love's most exalted need.

If you would give yourself to love, give all your tears and laughter to this life you have been gifted.

Stretch your tolerance to embrace the tenderness in all beings as your own.

Suffer gladly for one unbound moment of mercy, that you may rise above the walls that separate the sacred from the profane and transcend into the light that shines on all, demons and saints alike.

And know that you are here for this alone.

HOMECOMING

Shaking with rapture, I leaned against a wall to steady myself in contemplation.

"I am forever grateful to the generous spirit that blesses me.

And I would be content, but this unfolding mystery is more unsettling than the storms that laid waste my dreams.

What is this obsession that has me passing hours in dialogue with my inner self?

This yearning has raised me from misery and guided each step of my ascension. The same power that rebuilds my dreams puts a spring in my step and a song in my heart.

But who is the I that sings?

Am I in servitude to a lofty destiny I have yet to fully appreciate? Am I the prophet of old returning

with a sacred assignment, or a clever fox casting a net of illusions?

Would I be such a fool to chase my tail and grow dizzy in such fantasies? But would I refuse such a mission if truly offered? And is it merely a doubting fear that hinders me now?

In what depth of contentment can I rest unless I find the answers to these preposterous questions?"

Bewildered, I journeyed across the globe to an ancient monastery high in the mountains of Lebanon, where I hoped to unravel this mystery of the ethereal presence speaking with such passion through me.

From the Mediterranean Sea, a winding trail hugged the edge of a deep canyon as it climbed ever higher to the distant village of Bsharri, nestled between mountains like a rare jewel on the bosom of the earth. At the road's lofty apex, constrained between towering granite peaks and steep canyon cliffs, the monastery lay suspended between worlds.

As I approached, stone walls emerged from the surrounding forest that led me into a subterranean cavern and to the tomb of Kahlil Gibran.

It was evening by the time I reached the monastery, and I was left alone to sit in meditation.

Exhausted by the long journey to this ancient land, I relaxed. Closing my eyes, I sank into the inner realm.

In the silence, a familiar spiritual presence enveloped me. I couldn't name it or remember precisely when I'd been here before, but my soul knew this monastery, and my bones could feel that I belonged.

Here I was—a perfect stranger in a strange and distant land—home again.

My tears flowed with joy, and I cried out:

"This night in Bsharri, the mountains of Lebanon sleep in silence.

But not I.

Even here, in the home of my deeper self, my mind has me weighing my thoughts.

Why did I come? What is this need that follows me from city, through valley, to mountaintop?

This hunger is unrelenting; even in fullness I find no peace.

The fascination of my youth has grown into an enigma that gives me no rest.

I have lived and learned to trust the flow of nature, but still this need has me probing the pond with my staff.

With tireless patience, my soul awaits my surrender, but I would rather be a solver of riddles and puzzles.

Yet my folly is in my search, for my seeking mind goes on agitating the surface, thus prolonging its pursuit, while my depth smiles in silence.

If I must search, let my search begin in surrender to the perfect peace within, for is not peace the most precious treasure and all others nothing without her blessing?

To be intimate with my soul, I must be patient and release my burden.

Let me put down the staff and linger long enough for the pond to settle. Perhaps then I may meet my true self emerging from the depths."

I left the monastery and walked to my room in the midnight darkness.

My eyes were heavy and my senses hazy as I laid my body to rest. I cast one lone vision seed into the wishing well of my night-bound soul and surrendered my mind to its source.

AWAKENING

I slept in peace until dawn when an enticing scent perfumed the room.

The thin alpine air was thick with love's presence, and a fresh hint of spirit rode the wind.

My eyes opened momentarily to a beautiful sunrise reflected off the mountains outside. The curtains gently moved as the prophet's spirit entered my open window and sat at the foot of my bed. The familiar melody of his voice sang to me:

Before daybreak clears the fog of night, and the heavy mist lifts behind your closed eyelids;
Before vision turns from the inner realms to cast its gaze on the outer distance;
Let your awakening start within.
Weed out thorns of doubt that have entwined with the tender sprouts of love.

There is no reason to despair. For every problem, you hold countless solutions.

All that is awaits your notice.

And all that you can be lingers until your awakening.

You live in the dream that is being born each moment.

Your thoughts call forth miracles from nothingness.

Let this be your awakening.

You are the authority that invokes all that matters. Only you grant meaning, beauty, and love.

And who deserves your love less or more? Do not all colors of the rainbow come from the same invisible source? Seen through eyes of love, all is one grand tapestry woven together with threads of beauty.

Awake! I am here with you.

Together we polished the mirror of your psyche that you may feel me gazing upon you with affection.

You are keen now to turn on the light of consciousness. Your mind is eager to embrace higher visions, and your heart is yearning to surrender to deeper love.

Now watch as I transform you into my likeness.

My eyes opened from a slumber deeper than sleep as I crawled out from under the covers of my psyche on the soft bed of belonging.

A kiss of naked truth tenderly touched my deepest vulnerability with the sweetest satisfaction and in a burst of tears and laughter my senses rose into a transpersonal awareness. As I gazed long and deep through enlightened eyes, inner dimensions emerged in the stillness of my gaze.

My sense of separate self evaporated into pure spirit while my flesh dissolved like an iceberg melting into the vast ocean of our soul's warmth.

Held effortlessly in the luminous abyss of oneness, I witnessed the remnants of our scattered lives passing like ghosts between the mirrors of life and death until all our fragmented moments merged into one murmuring prayer.

I can barely speak of our spiritual source, for all the light of our soul is but a shadow upon its face. Yet from this we come and return inseparable as night and day, forever renewed.

From mystery into mystery upon mystery our whispering spirit breathes life into our soul and as a choir of countless voices dressed in forever lasting presence we are reborn again and again for the sheer wonder of it all.

REMEMBRANCE

Morning songbirds celebrated my awakening as I left my room to explore the small village of Bsharri.

A silent memory visited me like a passerby glancing momentarily through my open window. As I entered the town square, déjà vu struck. I saw children of yesteryear playing there.

A gentle, unseen hand brushed my shoulder with a startling familiarity. Turning, I looked in every direction with an exhilarating shiver that intensified when the reminiscent echo of my brother's voice whispered from somewhere:

Welcome home, Hajjar.

I listened, my senses stretched into space, waiting for truth to appear.

Fleeting sensations gathered like pieces of a puzzle, hinting impressions of a picture long forgotten.

Confused by the convolution of time, alone among strangers in the faintly familiar village, I scurried up the steep streets to gain a higher perspective.

I perched overlooking the small village with the towering cathedral and random buildings sprawled along wandering paths high in the alpine forest. Gazing over the expansive vista toward the Mediterranean, a tender love for this foreign place engulfed my senses.

I felt my mother's presence embracing the earth and sky as the aroma of cinnamon and mint invoked memories of her cooking. I heard her voice within my heart:

Welcome home, dear.

I was then enticed from my trance by a man waving a greeting from the street below. I followed him to a refrigerated storehouse where he invited me to taste apples and pears grown in nearby orchards.

Gazing into an apple like a crystal ball, I saw a candlelit room from my forgotten childhood. I sensed my brother's spirit, my mother's love, and my father's pride.

The first bite released a burst of nectar into my mouth; the crisp succulence answered a lifelong hunger for this forgotten sweetness.

The man asked of America with a zealous long-ing to belong to such a fairytale land of freedom. I replied:

"My friend, you and I are of the same soil.

Our desire for freedom would carry us away into our fantasies, yet our roots that bind us to this earth produce fruit much sweeter than any dream can be.

You are a man with roots in this sacred ground.

From the harvest of your toil, you give of your-self.

I am a seeker of silence, searching for the secrets of our soul.

My labor has unearthed more loving respect for you.

Your life may seem simple and distant from the dreams that stir in the solitude of your heart.

But your silent strength, like the spirit in these mountains, holds up the sky where all our dreams are but passing clouds."

Bidding the man farewell, I was irresistibly drawn toward the cathedral.

My feet, knowing more than my mind could fathom, carried me up timeworn steps to an open archway.

Standing there on the threshold to the cathe-dral, I slipped through the corridors of time. Thick smoke rose from burning incense and swirled into phantoms of another era. The chanting of bygone ages reverberated to the throb of my racing heartbeat.

As my father would have, I put my hand on the back of a wooden pew to guide myself to sit in meditation.

From a primal yearning, I realized for the first time that my life was a recurring dream, repeating a primordial struggle between fear and love.

Suddenly, as though my eyes were seeing light for the first time, I had a flashback of myself sitting here between my father and my mother. I remembered the figures in the stained-glass windows portraying the tale of Christ's persecution. I remembered the golden offering plates on the marble altar and the rows of candles dripping like tears that release our prayers to the heavens.

Amidst the chaos of bewildering memories, a translucent light filled the cathedral, and my inner vision carried me through the roof to a cherished memory. In my mind's eye, I saw a natural cathedral of rock precipices at the edge of a mountain meadow where a babbling brook sang a welcome song to my trembling heart. My eyes opened wide in shocking memory of this favorite place from my former childhood.

Quietly, but quickly, I left the cathedral and followed my instincts to the secret sanctuary hidden somewhere in the nearby mountains.

The limb of a cypress, moved by the wind, beckoned me onward. A faint figure appeared and then disappeared into the shadows of the forest, and I followed.

Everything in that enchanted place vibrated like cello strings beneath the bow of a master. Time carried me with ethereal grace over rocks and ravines into the late afternoon, each step planting a prayer for the events that followed. My pace quickened with anticipation as I climbed high into a narrow alpine meadow surrounded by majestic snowcapped peaks.

To the far end of the meadow I followed my mounting exhilaration toward the sound of water falling behind walls of stone where a column of mist swirled upward, evaporating into iridescent rainbows.

In this shimmering solarium, I stepped through a threshold between worlds.

The elementals invoked subtle realms of awareness in my mindstream. From beyond the veneer of reality, a choir of voices and trumpets proclaimed my return to this sanctuary of beauty. Spirits, dressed in flowing radiance, danced around me like leaves caught in the delicate embrace of a whirlwind. This wellspring of inspiration was concealed beyond the distance of a lifetime.

As I entered nature's temple with outstretched arms, my weakening knees brought me to the ground, humble to receive this honored blessing.

Rays of dazzling sunlight off the cascading waterfall synchronized with lightning flashes of remembrance. Clouds of forgetfulness burst with a thunderous shout from deep within my belly. And memory upon memory of my former life rained down upon my thirsty soul.

Intoxicated under the influence of this revelation of life beyond death, my feelings took flight in that moment to join with hidden moments of a generation long past.

Reuniting with this sacred site, my eyes flowed like fountains of joy, and I cried out in ecstasy:

"O beautiful home of my deepest love,

For so long you hovered in the silent space between my dreams.

Now I stand here on the lofty summit of glory, staggering in the light of my clandestine past.

If you will, emancipate my senses that I may see and hear all things secret."

Then in the stillness between heartbeats, I was lifted between worlds held apart by the lapse of time. I sailed the firmament through vast domains of light, undulating through seascapes of immaculate splendor. I saw eternity unveiled to the untold possibilities that await their moment of manifestation.

In that instance, the scattered elements of creation gathered again into a lucid image of the prophet shimmering in the mist of the waterfall. As though a force in his being directed my will, I was compelled to rise and walk toward him.

When I stood a short distance before him, he spoke:

I called you here to this home of your remembrance.

Long was the interlude of your absence from your homeland; and behold, you stand before me in flesh, and I am overjoyed that you followed my beckoning.

For a time between death and birth, silent and unaware of the seasons, your form lay in the bos-

om of the earth while your spirit dwelled in the heavens. You looked down from the windows of the constellations, and you envied humanity's sweet pleasures and mortal pains.

You were a songbird imprisoned in silence, and you yearned through the nights to sing your love songs again to the days.

Thus your longing was wrought from the dust of the earth to again face the sun.

Now your roots grow deep into the ground that bore you, and you ascend high into boundless realms where wisdom gathers like rain into thought.

The seeds of your yesterdays have blossomed.

The fruit of ages has fermented into sparkling soul wine, the harvest of patience.

This is our day of celebration.

I asked, "How is it that you know me more than I know myself?"

And the prophet answered:

You and I are one in spirit.

We were born together; but through birth, you were born into forgetfulness, and it is my will that you remember.

I came and died as your brother to call you home.

Thus, I play upon your weakness to evoke your strength.

I cast you in darkness that you might search for your light.

I move within you, urging you to reach always higher that you might remember me.

You feel my pulse in your heart, or else you would not stand here before me now.

I am ever ready to satisfy your hunger with love and to quench your thirst with wisdom.

And if this day is not a fulfillment of your need, then it remains still a promise.

If aught is left unsung, then we shall commune again tomorrow, and you shall drink from my fountain to your heart's content.

As you sleep, I whisper forgotten secrets to you, and because the trace of my genes flows in your veins, you remember.

You know now the cosmos in your stillness; when you part your lips, the voice of life comes forth from the authority that moves the heavens.

And forever on, you shall continue your way with my flame burning in your breast.

Though your needs change with the seasons, my constant love remains dressed in ways that answer your intrinsic need. But you alone must step naked into your heart's freedom.

Come closer now, unbind yourself, and surrender to the silence where together we are one.

I undressed and stepped through the cloud of vibrant mist into the liquid curtain pouring down upon me.

Amidst the deafening roar of the crashing deluge, all I could hear was the soundless voice of spirit, singing this message of love to humanity:

Forget not that you dwell with me always, a boundless drop in a boundless sea.

There is no end to my source, nor limit to my grace.

When you drift into sleep, I hold you in silent serenity.

And when you awaken, it is within my presence that you dwell.

I live in your heart and you live in mine.

You are my dream and I am your awakening.

Through you, I am dressed in beauty.

Through me, you are beyond what can be.

The evening was late.

One by one, minutes passed as the earth turned her back toward the sun.

Again, day gathered up her radiance to welcome in the night.

As the familiar shadows of darkness wrapped themselves around me, I smiled.

Knowing that all is sacred and—

Without End.

NOTE

I refer to Kahlil Gibran as my great-uncle for lack of a better word to describe our kinship.

I met with Wahib Keyrouz, the curator of the Kahlil Gibran museum in Bsharri, Lebanon, to study the Gibran family tree and clarify my relation to Kahlil. The records go back many generations to five Gibran brothers who each produced an expansive family branch.

Kahlil and I are each a leaf on separate branches of the same family tree.

ACKNOWLEDGMENTS

Writing this book has drawn me deeper into the great mystery. Through dreamy synchronicities, past inklings somehow emerged from the womb of nothingness into the poetic magic on these pages, and I am an amazed witness.

My deepest gratitude goes to the all-providing spirit that enables me to play in this magical realm.

I extend warm appreciation to the multitude of people who helped me give birth to this book: Lumyai Bonmai, Armand Altman, Gila Kuhlmann, Irene Hage, Elizabeth Rygard, Robert Zenk, Ian Baker, Dik Darnell, Dorie Cofer, Gladys Haggar, Michelle Hansen, Maja Kasdan, Job Smulders, Maja Thuna, John Chatteris, Laura Moorehead, Bharat Rochlin, Shayla Spencer, Arjuna Noore, Zosia Sims,

ACKNOWLEDGMENTS

Jim Channon, Ann Ekeberg, John Schreiner, Dave Dawson, Simon Brunsdon, Nathon Crystal, Laura Eliseo, Neil Beechwood, Tony Krantz, Joel Haggar, Jonah Ross, Ariana Satayathum, Natalia Hojny, and Arvid Schwenk.

To my agents Greg Dinkin, Frank Scatoni, and Whitney Lee.

To my editors Lindsay Brown, Henry Covey, Julie Steigerwaldt, and Ali McCart. To Alex Chubotin for his wonderful illustrations.

And to all the folks at Beyond Words and Simon & Schuster, especially my publishers Cynthia Black and Richard Cohn. Thank you all for your part in making this dream come true.